The Light Holds

The Light Holds

POEMS BY

Harvey Shapiro

Wesleyan University Press
Middletown, Connecticut

Acknowledgment is gratefully made to the following periodicals and
newspapers in which many of the poems in this book were first published:
The Atlantic: "Things Seen," "Getting Through the Day"; *Beyond
Baroque:* "Summer and Back," "May 14, 1978"; *Confrontation:*
"Blue Eyes," "Causing Anguish," "Experiences"; *Epoch:* "From the
Greek Anthology," "Brooklyn Heights," "City"; *Forthcoming:* "Cityscape,"
"Sons," "Borough Hall," "The End"; *Forum:* "After the Love-making";
The Hudson Review: "At the Shore"; *Images:* "Winter Sun"; *The Jewish
Daily Forward:* 'Learning"; *The Nation:* "Cummings," "Interlude,"
"Discovery"; *New York Arts Journal:* "Battlements," "How It Happened,"
"The Gift of Remembering"; *Paris Review:* "On a Sunday"; *Partisan Review:*
"The Card," "The Wish"; *Pequod:* "Memorial Day," "Movie"; *Plainsong:*
"July"; *Poetry:* A Jerusalem Notebook"; *Sun:* "Middle Class," "Bad News,"
"Age." "The Twig" was first published in *A Treasury of Yiddish Poetry,* edited
by Irving Howe and Eliezer Greenberg.

All inquiries and permissions requests should be addressed to the
Publisher, Wesleyan University Press, 110 Mt. Vernon Street, Middletown,
Connecticut 06457

Distributed by Harper & Row Publishers, Keystone Industrial Park,
Scranton, Pennsylvania 18512

Library of Congress Cataloging in Publication Data

Shapiro, Harvey.
The light holds.

I. Title.
PS3537.H264L5   1984   811'.52   83-23339
ISBN 0-8195-5097-3 (alk. paper)
ISBN 0-8195-6096-0 pa. (alk. paper)

Manufactured in the United States of America

First printing, 1984; second printing, 1984

Contents

1

2

3

4

I

Things Seen

There is no natural scenery like this:
when her loose gown from her shoulders
falls, the light hardens, shadows
move slowly, my breath catches.

The flame of the blue cornflower,
a half inch above the flower,
fanned by wind.

From the Greek Anthology

Darling, start at any point you wish.
How kind I was to myself in those days,
and so happy cataloguing ships.

Your lovely way of walking and the radiance of
  your face.
The Cyprian goddess set these before me.
The rest I accomplished on my own.

The Twig

From the Yiddish of Joseph Rolnick

A man plants a stick,
pats the dirt
and says, Mine.
Now he is committed,
let him pray for sun and rain.
Each night he covers miles
for the sake of that naked twig,
and in the morning
runs to it as fast.
He is worn out with worry
and waits for his last days.
But how that stick
branches in his mind—
a mighty tree,
full of shade,
where years later he can sit
in the middle of the day
as the sun grows warm.

July

You poets of the Late T'ang send me messages
    this morning.
The eastern sky is streaked with red.
Linkages of bird song make a floating chain.
In a corner of the world, walled in by ocean
    and sky,
I can look back on so many destructive days
    and nights,
and forward too, ego demons as far as
    mind reaches.
Here, for a moment, the light holds.

May 14, 1978

The poet Kenji Miyazawa asks me,
What world is it you want to enter?
Percussive rain on the early morning window.
The house, the steady breathing, focused now
on the lighted surface of my desk.
I cannot answer him for joy and dread.

City

Silver dawn over Madison Avenue.
The refrigerator shuts softly, like a kiss.

He is dying of the terminal cutesies
she says of the cultural journalist,
the newspaper spread before her on the table.
Thousands fail in her sight daily.

The word "happiness"
like the sun in late March
is a light I can see
but not feel. There it is
on the back of my hand
as real as my hand
clenched now
against the wind on 48th Street.

In Great Neck, at 4:30 in the morning,
Ring Lardner and Scott Fitzgerald
walk the streets. American success
is their theme. The sleepers drink it in
across the lawns.

In the lamp's circle,
warmed by bourbon,
I play the role out. It is
not to tell the world
anything. What is it
the world would want to know?

Her furious body, plunged into sleep.
On the pillow, her live hair,
helmet and cloak. What I say in the room
is for me and the walls. We are doing darkness,
each in his own way.

The Card

Closed in by the rain, the February chill,
he looks at her card sent from an island
in the sun. She writes, "The vasts and deeps
of the mistakenness of this undertaking
remain to be measured." What he drinks
can't begin to fill his emptiness
or banish the chill. Only the pen seems warm.
Is she warning him of her vision of their
condition? Possibly. She writes,
"I'm having funny dreams, you and I
in Paris. Also you and my mother
married. And others." When she comes back
he will begin to batter at her indifference
again. She does not sign love, just
"Pray for me" and the initial of her name.

The Wish

This night in Brooklyn is as ancient
as nights get, though the moon
hangs like a lamp, and the traffic
slurs in my room.
My desire is as sharp as whiskey
or a hurt nerve, from my head
to my hand: to populate
the void, to turn this blankness
into a field of stars, where I can sleep
forever in my earned sleep,
comforted by the wind off Atlantic
Avenue, and the waters at its end.
Lights rise from the water, a City
across the way, that I raise
in my empty room to starlight.

Middle Class

Whatever happened to the screaming-meemies?
I see my life has surfaced once again.
She explained to me on the phone
all the things I had to live for.
It came to three items. Not enough.
I spent one hour with one son at his shrink
discussing (my choice) why he seemed
      to hate me.
Because I'm insensitive and unfeeling, he said.
The shrink said it wasn't hate but anger.
We all agreed to discuss it again.
If I get up when the alarm rings tomorrow,
I can pay for the hour and all the hours.
On the subway I see nobody finds it easy.
As beautiful as you are, you're not enough.

Learning

He is back in a student's room
having learned nothing
in 35 years, except
despair and happiness are sweeter
to him now, they are purer
to his taste, as if he had
learned to discriminate among
his emotions, to say this is
despair and this is happiness.

2.

Paying dues—
you imagine this is
a creative loneliness.
You are aware of wind
or traffic rushing in
the street. You think
God is as lost as you:
the fixed points vanished,
the beginning and the end
both forgotten. Day
after day the light
is its own explanation.

3.

In my room a bug climbs the white wall
or rather seems to be thinking of climbing it.
I too would like to get to the top of something.

4.

Rabbi Nachman's final message:
Gevalt! Do not despair!
There is no such thing as despair at all!
Shouted from the very depths of the heart.

Reading

What does every man have?
Business and desire (such as it is),
said Hamlet. His business
and his desire made him sick.
So it is with many of us.

How does *Black Beauty* end?
The horse dies.
How does *Moby Dick* end?
The whale dies.
How does *Anna Karenina* end?
The woman dies.
How does *The Metamorphosis* end?
The bug dies.

When you climb out of it
and put boards across it
you can jump on those boards,
they have such resiliency.

San Francisco

In this western city, under cloud cover,
the lives are ranged about me on the hills,
no more obscure to me than in Manhattan.
Downtown, a writer gets up from his desk
to check the Bay Bridge and the white sails
against blue water. What is always there,
out the window, is the failure I feel
before America, my inability to make it rhyme
with my interior weather, except
under the stress of strong emotion—
love or loss—when I know
my father is stumbling home,
tired after work, carrying his family
in his heart to whom he promises
happiness and all bright things,
and he stops in a store
to bring me, sick in bed, a giant
locomotive to take me there.

Summer and Back

Pearl-gray dawn over the sea's margin.
A few terns against the lit sky to the east.

2.

Bird clickings in the sheltered grove.
Sky darkens with breeze, wind coming up
like a car. I stay out for the pleasure
of the first rain.

3.

On the wires, bird identification
like aircraft identification.
My life depends on it.

How the reaching back, over 30 years,
takes place effortlessly. Grace of memory,
though the affect is dolorous,
knits up the mind.

4.

Of the tunes that played in my head for you
the one that remains is Lord Randall's Lament.

5.

Closing your door
I feel some great erotic mystery
slipping away—
Phil Spitalny's All-Girl Orchestra,
the show over, descending
into the pit.

6.

Recognizing the real, as in the undersong
I heard when the blonde, with open throttle,
ran over "The Man I Love" and the backup
   pianist
with that genuine pallor of a man
who has never been outside by day
riffed through the pauses and the bourbon
tasted like it did 20 years ago.
As if the sentimental were not real. Starlight
after the neon of the roadhouse, a windshield
full of stars.

7.

Absolute blue bearing down on me
makes me swerve into thoughts of you.
That earth softness, wetness, foliage
thick enough to hide me in a room
like any other in the city.

8.

I come to you
as a poor man
comes to the table of the rich,
ill at ease
and determined
to enjoy it.

9.

In my fifties
I discovered fish too fierce
for my equipment. They took
all my bait. A bare hook
became my emblem.

Explanation

On whose authority
are these things being said?
On the authority of style.

On a Sunday

When you write something
you want it to live—
you have that obligation, to give it
a start in life.
Virginia Woolf, pockets full of stones,
sinks into the sad river
that surrounds us daily. Everything
about London amazed her, the shapes
and sights, the conversations on a bus.
At the end of her life, she said,
London is my patriotism.
I feel that about New York.
Would Frank O'Hara say, Virginia Woolf,
get up? No, but images from her novels
stay in my head—the old poet,
Swinburne, I suppose, sits on the lawn
of the country house, mumbling
into the sun. Pleased with the images,
I won't let the chaos of my life
overwhelm me. There is the City,
and the sun blazes on Central Park
in September. These people, on a Sunday,
are beautiful, various. And the poor
among them make me think
the experience I knew will be relived again,
so that my sentences will keep hold
of reality, for a while at least.

Age

Now he is 57
if you remove the words
the dry skin will hang
the eyes will dim
women will smell death.

In the kitchen the empties
stand at attention. We respect
each other, we recognize
each other. Kindlings
like the morning were what we sought.

Said my mother at 79
from her hospital bed,
Yesterday I was young;
today I am old; now I believe it.

This wood I write on
is so scarred,
it could of itself, by
its experience, pass
judgment on my life.

I hear the trucks
on the Brooklyn-Queens Expressway
heading into dawn.
What if I had it all
to do over again?

The terror felled me
once or twice,
as in the war.
Hunching forward,
I hear no cheers
as I approach the line.

Thursday

You failed presences,
I cannot name you
so I call you loss.

Heavy traffic. This man is crying
and that one raises his bloody stumps,
and my teeth grind the song to bits.

The way madmen must think
God set me on this earth
for something.

Discovery

When I wake
in the early hours
I think there must be
something I have learned from
these violent dreams
and then I know
how it will be in
my last hours.

2

The Gift of Remembering

Judy Handler's mother said
I looked like the butcher's son.
Peter Geiger, my rival,
died in the war. I survived,
flying over Germany, looking
more Jewish than ever.

The hard-boiled egg I eat
still has the sweet sustenance
of an egg taken from a glass jar
on a bar in Atlantic City
in 1945, the summer after
my war had ended, my missions done,
and the drinks all on the house,
whoever paid.

2.

Rain and a low sky bring the planes in close
though not as close as they came to our tents
in Italy, on dark days, friendly fighters
practicing their rolls, to tell the sleeping grounded
combat crews, this is the sound of friendly death.

3.

Fire on the rim of heaven.
Two bright stars off the wing, higher,
and the cities underneath,
cold, final blaze.

Memorial Day

I stretch in the crater of a dune,
mist carrying sun,
some 35 years from
Flak Alley, the punctured
sky over Vienna, Berlin.
An antique war
drifting through my head,
no more real now
than the Late Late Show.
I don't even tell
the stories any more. I don't
remember what death
was like. I can't even see
the dead crewmen.
Only enough memory left
to feel the sun.

Cummings

On May nights, in Patchin Place,
Greenwich Village of my memory,
girls from Smith and Vassar
vagabonding for the weekend,
lovely in the alley light,
would chant up to the shy poet's
window: How do you like your blue-
eyed boy, Mr. Death. And indeed
Buffalo Bill's defunct—pencil-thin
by the alley gate, sketch book in hand,
open collar of the artist, across
from the Women's House of Detention
in the waning light of afternoons.

Sons

They have what they want.
You're going down
but ready to help.

They touch you sometimes.

What to give them?
Vanish.
Leave a trace.

Autobiography

To read by daylight.
To look up and see
on my wall
the print of the plans
for the Brooklyn Bridge,
the pleasure of its being there
with the current of the East River
surging underneath. Stasis
and flow. Of course. The tension
of the New Critics still feeding
my fifties life.

Borough Hall

In Brooklyn I knew Louis Zukofsky
and George Oppen. I saw the Bridge
and the Statue of Liberty.
I had a wife, two sons, a house.
All this is recounted in my poems.

No horseman will
pass by my stone.
If I am to be remembered
let it be
by a young woman on the IRT
getting off at Borough Hall.

Years Ago

The sky was bright
blue—
the color of birds'
eggs in storybooks.
The print was so large
when my young sons talked.

Movie

At the space movie
the galaxies seemed so fine
viewed from aboard
the rocket ship. I didn't want
the trip to end. Out there,
I thought, we could move forever,
without consequence or pain,
just the sensation of flight
and precise tasks to be done.
Everyone on board
knew the story line meant nothing,
the dialogue just air,
pious remnants of an earthly life.

Around Town

And this is just your everyday pathos.
The handsome young woman
in the white turtleneck
leaves the guy at the table,
enters the phone booth
to cry, silently,
for maybe three minutes,
then dabs twice and returns.

Or the little black girl on the subway
to Brooklyn, clutching
a miniature white doll
in a matchbox cradle—
blond hair, blue eyes—
one hand around the box,
the thumb caressing.

For Whitman

The Statue of Liberty in the mist.
The Brooklyn Bridge sunk in gloom.
A ship from Ecuador
slides out of its berth,
shrill whistles from the tug.
Joggers in yellow slickers
dot the promenade.
You who come after me
will never see this.

Brooklyn Heights

1.

I'm on Water Street in Brooklyn,
between the Brooklyn Bridge
and the Manhattan Bridge,
the high charge of their traffic
filling the empty street.
Abandoned warehouses
on either side.
In the shadowed doorways, shades
of Melville and Murder Incorporated.
Five o'clock October light.
Jets and gulls in the fleecy sky.
Climbing the hill to Columbia Heights,
I turn to see the cordage
of the Brooklyn Bridge, and behind it
the battle-gray Manhattan.

2.

This room shelved high with books
echoes with my midnights. Pages
of useless lines swim in it. Only
now and then a voice cuts through
saying something right: No sound
is dissonant which tells of life.
The gaudy ensigns of this life
flash in the streets; a December light,
whipped by wind, is at the windows.
Even now the English poets are in the street,
Keats and Coleridge on Hicks Street,
heading for the Bridge. Swayed aloft there,
the lower bay before them, they can
bring me back my City line by line.

Winter Sun

Shakespeare in Central Park in winter,
bare ruined choirs behind him,
a green figure, in green livery,
clutching a book. Afternoon sun
no higher than the Gulf and Western
building. Rags of the departing year
in my head, the lived with
but not understood events that I
have worn thin through worry.
If only the imagination rayed from the bard's
head, from behind his sunken eyes—
if those eyes were zap guns of the imagination
transforming the unusable past into energy,
bunched light waves stronger than
this winter sun that shows me who I am
against bare trees and a sullen sky.

Bad News

1.

There is a bag lady who has her station
on 43rd Street near Sixth Avenue,
in the middle of the sidewalk. She was there
when I went to work, and there on my return.
The New York Times and *The New Yorker*
are on that street. So is the Century Club.
It's a hard street to impress, I want
to tell her, even with bags of different colors
and scarves to examine slowly in the sun.

2.

Death won't claim you. Nothing
as dramatic as that.
You'll just go off the edge, roll
off it, like falling out of bed.
They can tell from the sound.

3.

She opens for the telephone
more than for me.
The laughs keep getting
deeper, keep coming
and the breath...

4.

What can these clouds tell me—
I am so hooked on the day to day—
when they sail over
like lofty propositions.

5.

Subway cars roll in
each like a Gauguin jungle
with messages for the city
from the city: "This is
energy from my soul"
and "United Artists."

6.

The local prophet,
bearded, wearing skins in summer,
dropped a potted plant in the middle
of 79th Street and Madison Avenue
and walked on. Tires crunched
on the shards, and flowers
bloomed in the headlights.

7.

There are other realities
I keep telling the world.
Why do I rage when I say it?
Because there is the one reality
that I cannot bring myself to say.

8.

These stars have no significance.
As it turned out
I didn't know enough
to find my way home.

A Memorial

My mother and father on the town,
in the photograph. American jazz
in the swing of her handbag
banging from her wrist.
Spats, and the woman
with a rose in her hair.
Hey, this was
a big romance. He was making money,
going to make more money. Everything
was looking up.
I love them in this photograph.

Blue Eyes

Young women with the baby fat
still on them, smelling of milk.
Against that, her bravery—
striding out of bed in the morning,
her years, her children underfoot,
her blue eyes flashing warning.

"I could make some of these guys very happy,"
she said, looking up from the personals
in the *New York Review of Books*.

You read to her of war,
devastation, gut-chilling
insecurity, and her blue eyes
waver, and she sleeps
like an American child.

"Is this a peak experience?"
she said, sliding down beside him,
her blue eyes laughing at his desperate age.

Sound of surf through dense fog.
Moisture streaming from the screened windows.
"Where are the beautiful love poems?"
she keeps asking him.

She became the line
he had in his head
just before sleep, that
he thought he would retain
and now it's gone.

After the Love-making

After the love-making
in which we tasted each other
so that the colors spread and mixed
we got up quietly to prepare dinner.

The sadness of the year ending.
The dead outside my window,
that increasing company of relatives and friends.
So we are not to be herded into freight cars.
Each will have his chance at happiness.

To be able to help each other.
Is that possible?
At the end of the play
you say to me that the life we saw
has reverberations, has history.
I agree and want to say
that even our drama
is not merely personal,
though we see only the edge of the personal.
I am with you
in saying it is not enough.

Like Touch

Shadows of the leaves
in the high tree moving
across my closed lids
are like touch remembered.

Causing Anguish

That face
is dead in my eyes, dead as an empty theater,
which once meant festival, drinks
on the house, erotic fantasy time,
the Stones sending down
clusters of bright balloons from the rafters
of Madison Square Garden while
the girl in front waved her ass
and waved her ass.

Causing anguish. She never
saw herself that way.
Innocent bystander. As I am
in my life. Who is the one who suffers?
"These are ancient routines,"
as Wallace Stevens says
in another connection.

By her genital beard
I swear this is happiness.
Charles Laughton, eyes misted,
praising Rembrandt's wife. Her body
splayed against the universe,
spangled, star-glutted.

How It Happened

He told her his dream,
it was like talking to the sea.

That week had a lot of damage in it.

The family is the world in which he moved.
She laughed past midnight at the images.

In the streets of the city, other women
kept watch on him for her.

That week had a lot of damage in it.
Surveying the damage, he began to see
his life would always be like that.

Saturday

It is noon and you don't know
what to do with your life.
It always begins again,
so you wait for it to begin again.
Then come the songs, then comes
the bitterness, then comes
the glorious end.

It was a rhythmic vitality
in her laugh, her walk.
What else was I to do?
The way her eyes widen
is still with me. Shall I forget
the mystery of women because
I sleep alone?

Waking unhappy and alone
at two AM is the way
you wanted to be. You can
put on the light.
There's no one to disturb.
That taste in your mouth
is your dream:
infidelity, cowardice, fear.
The way God wanted me to be,
I cry, opening me up,
feeling through the soft entrails
for a few hard grains of truth.

A heroic deception, learned
from Levine (for whom it may
be true), but as for you, you
like the gloom and the taste
in your mouth, you choose it
and you call it life.

Interlude

He had his own prescription for entering
the life of his times.
This was what everything drifted to,
inexorably: His hand
on the small of her back.

She spoke about the special
loneliness of the city.

She said, lay down your arms, nothing
will come of this but more tears, more
unhappiness, on which you fatten and grow dull.
Enjoy the streets. The rain is
your proper element. Stop trying to light fires
where damp ashes are what is meant.

Goddess, destroyer, flaming-haired,
whiskey-throated,
the small birds keep their distance
when you walk across to me.

Song

It was as if she had brought the cooling rain,
the breeze through the curtained window,
the taste of the bourbon,
so that I turned to the street again,
happy in the traffic and the rain.

3

At the Shore

If my head is numb,
my heart, my genitals also,
I can guard my wallet
confidently in the subway
like a citizen.

When the face that was beautiful
turns ugly in argument—
You always—
then it is I see that death will come
leaving me as ignorant as ever.

The bugs batting against the lamp, the midges,
in an old house, in summer,
the peacefulness after voices are stilled
is like the still small voice we were
told to tune in to as children.

If you could figure it out,
the domestic arrangements you fall into,
like beds or a summer at the shore.
You wake up facing a meadow,
beyond that water, beyond that an island.
On the other side of the island
you begin another life.

5.

The big dipper is outside my door,
so I can find my way north,
if that is the way I need to go.
For the moment I am content
to drink and smoke and stroke
the inside of your thighs
that have taken on the smoothness
of beach glass, glazed by the sea,
a remembrance.

6.

The man who has no talent for relationships
listens to the wind. It comes sweeping off
the harbor and the bay into the blue room.
He thinks he can recognize
every tune it plays. What
he wants is merciless music, the sound
at the very bottom of the harbor.

7.

The chink of the moth
on my glass, the dog's
heavy breathing as if
some race were being run again,
and my own solitary presence
at my desk are all emblems
for me of the night world.
In the next room
you sprawl in sleep
so that my day can begin again.

8.

Night after night
the wind is from the south,
off Shelter Island, wisps
of lightning play about the sky.
Orienting myself by that speaking wind,
I rise, troubled in lamplight,
to say once again that my
dreams are pernicious
and blur the clarity of what I see—
mute swans, cormorants, the rushes.
This self, this consciousness, this pressure cooker
for rhetoric and bad vibes
that I lug to the country.
It is my usual hour—3 AM.
When I was younger and had the gift of sight
I did not understand that all that is asked
is that we not mar the work of creation,
doing injury to others and ourselves.

Time Off

Sunday morning—too much metropolitan
poetry in the park: the ecology freak
in purple handing out leaflets
on how to beat AT&T, the folk-dancing
group clomping around to what must be
Ballin' the Jack. Aimless in Manhattan,
I enjoy the ruins of my desk.
My one moment of illumination
came Saturday morning, about nine o'clock,
in bed with beauty. It has to take me
through a long weekend and a short life.

How It Is with Me

In my luxuriant cool,
after a bit of weed and
a little coffee, I go out
among the moving slim waists
of the Upper East Side.

Getting Through the Day

The old woman
humming, coming
up the subway steps,
one hum
for each step.

Battlements

For H. R. Hays

These dark colors I place against
the blue heron at Louse Point. Summer
eternal, though after we go,
it may all be paved over.

Into the calm morning
steps the blue heron. The shore
oscillates like a nest to his leaving.

The old poet is brought down to look at the bay.
He thinks he has never done justice to anything
    in his poems.
Gulls crack shells on the macadam road.
Returning, held by others, he urinates by the car.

When you die, who will come out
to meet you if not the blue heron.

For William Dunbar and His Lament

Sir, the words have prevailed, though readers
  are few.
In the early morning I lament with you, and take
  comfort from you
that some have found the way to fix their name.
In your trim stanzas, noble in their naming
  of others,
you hold fast to light, and are access to light
  for others,
for me, in this darkness I cannot strike or leave.

Memento Mori

Suppose you lived across from a funeral home—
say the Frank E. Campbell funeral home
where the stacked dead wait to be delivered
like fresh loaves of bread—would you,
   each night,
when you rise to the muted windows
look on that day as the last day

but know it is not for you to make
the judgment, it is enough to believe
the judgment is done, sleep peacefully
on that, rise tomorrow as the sun
touches with light the streets and avenues
where you go in search of your life.

Considering

Like the man who walked
his three-legged dog
in Central Park—
pride and pathos
struggling in his face—
I consider my life
and my art.

Cityscape

The self hurt, humiliated,
has no recourse but to the world.
Dawn's light
on the streets, though
the buildings are still dark.

Sparrows nesting in the hollow crossbar
of the traffic light. A beak
and head emerge, and then the line
of flight, as if city air
could sustain flight.

June and the hum of air conditioners
fills the side streets.
A poster in a Madison Avenue boutique
says Poverty Sucks. The crowd
coming out of the Whitney opening
believes it, so well kept
they shine along the pavement.

Gulls as far inland
as Fifth Avenue.

After the garbage truck
has stopped grinding the world,
the rhetoric inside my head
catches and begins to work.

My eye on the cityscape,
nervous, alert,
as I move through
the day. No part
of the surface
is neutral ground.

The End

Imagine your own death.
I'm wearing my father's
gray tweed overcoat.
I've just had a corned-beef
sandwich on 47th Street

(I asked for lean
and it came fat,
I should have sent it
back) when it hits me
in the chest.

Experiences

"I've been there before!"
shouted like the prophet
when he was lifted up
to behold the burning city
but I was going down
into the subway for my
first vision of the day.

In the hospital I heard a voice say,
"The chart has to accompany the patient,"
which used to be true in our universe
when Kafka wrote and Jews prayed.

When I was mugged
and kicked in the head
by three stalwart blacks
I felt like a gazelle
cut out from the herd
on the deserted subway platform.

In summer I place my one plant
outside. That makes the apartment
seem so bare. But the plant gets spiky,
luminous, and cheers me when
I see it from my bedroom window.
We are beginning to help
each other understand what it is to be
solitary but alive.... False poetry.
Still, the plant is a kind of teacher
as I am a beginning student.

Seeing old friends, or even people we've known
a long time who are not friends, simply
people who share a part of our past,
is healing, heals the discontinuities,
permits us to believe that our lives
have grown organically, from there to here,
and that we have not existed in isolated
moments, as different people, caught
in different stories, moving at different speeds,
which is the way we know it to have been.

In my apartment everything
suggests the emptiness of Grant's tomb
figuring Grant got out
and nobody got in.

I don't panic any more
when I wake in the small hours.
I know this time is as real
as any other.

Wanting to make barge music by the Brooklyn Bridge
the way other men want to make love, or be happy,
or take something home to the wife and kids.

Not having known any other life,
this is what one summons.
There is sympathetic understanding,
but the mind is locked in place
by its experience.

He keeps saying "these streets"
and doesn't know
what he means.

The literature of our time, like papers
pushed into the cracks of the wall in Jerusalem,
to be read by an unknown god, when he
returns to consciousness and summons us.

The light streaming from the closed door
of the one letter of the alphabet
I am supposed to say.

4

A Jerusalem Notebook

A city of ascensions,
nowhere to go but up.
Forcing the spirit in New York
is the commonplace, we live
there as if we were in Jerusalem,
Jesus and Mohammed touching down
and going up, just another
launching pad, as I get off
the bus and head home.

Postcard
It is not far from here
that the parents stood
and the child, placed into the priest's machine,
heard the wail
of Moloch. And the bronze god,
arms outstretched, smiled at the smoke.
Two of the kings of Judah
burned their sons here—
Hell, Gehenna, Gai Hinnom,
the pleasant valley of Hinnom,
pink, scarred and silent
in the fading light.

3.

If you begin housekeeping
at the edge of Gehenna
you have to expect a little trouble.
She said to me: I like
this place because there are no birds.
No. She said to me: *Actually,*
I like this place because there
are no birds. The white lizard
on the white wall seemed transfixed
by the thought of hell. Looking east
and south I see the Judean hills,
a desert like a sea.
Or dunes dropping off into a sea.
Morning vapors rising off the land.
Give me this place for my own,
I cried, and I will live here forever.
The prospect is as sweet
as a Sabbath morning. Across
the valley of Gehenna cypresses line
the sloping hill. I can walk
there any time I like, now
I am old enough, and look back
on this life I have begun.

4.

Tourists
She is crying over three olives
that I threw out. Three olives
but my food, she cries. She is
not a child but a woman.
Outside Zion Gate, Jaffa Gate,
Dung Gate, she rubs my arm slowly.
Gates excite her. Where I come in
at night, the city is so beautiful.

5.

It is the temple mount.
It is a little like the temple mount,
though I myself constitute
the sightseers, worshippers,
and sometimes the visiting god.

6.

Whatever brought me here, to a new moon
over Zion's hill, dark moon
with the thin cusp silvered,
help me believe in my happiness, for
it was guilt that woke me. A voice
on the telephone crying breakdown.
Illusions of my own ego causing destruction
while outside the marvelous
machinery of day has opened, light
traffic on the road to the citadel.
And as I look again, it is all
swept clean, except for
a faint pink in the sky and on the old
stones of the city, and language in my head
that I brought with me, that I carry,
that I use to mark my way.

7.

My way of being in the world:
not perfect freedom or the pitch
of madness, but that the particulars
of my life become manifest
to me walking these dark streets.

8. *For C. R.*

When I dropped permanence from my back
and saw what I had taken for
solid buildings and good roads
was desert all about me and within me,
how bright became the sunlight,
how sweet the evening air.

9. *The Old Jewish Poet Floats in the Dead Sea*

It is the lowest place on earth
but he has been lower.
For example, he has been on the heights
of Massada, watching the Roman soldiers
jack off in the baths below.
He knows his turn will be next.
Beneath him floats a crow.
Beneath the crow floats the crow's shadow.
Beneath the crow's shadow is another Jew.
These Judean junk hills
fill his head with sulphur.
Every hill is a hill of skulls.

10.

I understand we are like smoke.
It streams from my cigar into the morning air,
silken, prismlike in sunlight
as I sit by the window.
Nothing I do with my life
could be as beautiful.

11.

Lizard lines in his skin.
Striving to become one with the stones
like the lizard, even as the pen
darts into the shadow of the page.

12.

I have dreams coming out of my ears,
she said. Why not? This city has seen
so many mad dreamers, their stale dreams
even now looking for new homes.
The stones dream in the sun,
the lizards. In the golden mosque,
riots of line and color, shapes dream
in the marble columns, pulsing in
and out of sleep. When the city wakes
the action is brief and bloody.
Let it sleep. Let the gabardined Jews
dream of the Messiah. He approaches
the blocked-off gate of the walled city.
Taste the dream of the Jews.

13.

Why did I want to sit out all the time,
was the air so special? Yes,
soft and today dust-blue. But the smell
of corpses had been everywhere, and more
   to come.
Red buses and blue buses raced the roads
to the small towns, carrying infant Jesuses,
dynamite. Blondes from Scandinavia,
silver-toed, tried on Arab dresses
while the man in the stall scratched his crotch.
It was all happening inside the city.
And at the edge was desert.

14.

Middle East music on the radio: Hebrew
   love songs,
Arab wails. Carmel Dry Gin
taking me up Zion's hill.
Lights on the stones of the ancient city.

15.

Who needs more happiness? People living
on the edge (of pain, of death,
of revelation) need time in the sun,
a lengthening interval between
the sonic boom and the rattled glass.

16.

I cannot dissever my happiness from language
or from your body. Light a candle for me
at the false tomb of David, I am of that line.
Let the young scarecrow who might be from
    47th Street
say a blessing for me. Sway over the candle's
    flame
like the old Arab riding toward me on his donkey.
If I forget my happiness, let me be dust.
Jerusalem, here I am going up again.
It is your moon, your labyrinths, your desert
crowding east where the sun waits.

About the Author

A native of Chicago and a graduate of Yale and
Columbia universities, Harvey Shapiro was for eight
years the editor of the *New York Times Book Review.* He
is now deputy editor of the *Times Sunday Magazine*
and a *Times* literary critic. He has published six books
of poetry, including *Battle Report* (Wesleyan, 1966) and
This World (Wesleyan, 1971). He lives in New York City.

About the Book

The Light Holds has been composed in Linotron 202
Galliard by Carolinatype. It was printed on 60 lb.
Warren's Olde Style. It was printed and bound at
Kingsport Press. The jackets and covers were printed
by New England Book Components. It was designed
and produced by Joyce Kachergis Book Design and
Production.